Let's Visit Seoul

Text by Suzanne Crowder Han · Illustrations by Kim Mi-on

Seoul has been the capital of Korea since the late fourteenth century when Yi Sŏng-gye, King T'aejo, the first king of the newly established Chosŏn Dynasty(1392-1910), chose it as the most propitious site on the Korean Peninsula to build his new capital, which he called Hanyang.

Of course the city has undergone much change and growth since 1394. The population now exceeds ten million, or about one hundred times its population in the time of King T'aejo, and the city has expanded far beyond the city wall he constructed. However, just as it was then, it is still the center of Korea's government, economy, culture and society. Moreover, it is now known worldwide as one of the most exciting cities in Asia.

Journey with Kurt and Elise as they explore the sights and sounds of Seoul, a city steeped in history, a city both ancient and modern, a city of constant change.

1394년 이성계가 새 왕조인 조선(1392-1910)을 세우면서 한반도에서 가장 상서로운 곳으로 현재의 서울을 한양이라 칭하며 왕조의 수도로 삼았습니다. 그 후 서울은 한국의 정치, 경제, 사회, 문화의 중심지로 성장과 발전을 계속하여 인구 천만이 넘는 세계적인 도시가 되었습니다.

커트와 엘리스가 서울의 이모저모를 찾아가 볼 것입니다. 고색창연하면서도 현대적인 도시 서울, 이 축복의 도시를 그들과 함께 여행하시기 바랍니다.

Copyright ⓒ 1993 by Hollym Corporation; Publishers · All rights reserved · First published in 1993 · Sixth printing, 2005 by Hollym International Corp.
at 18 Donald Place, Elizabeth, NJ 07208, USA · Tel: (908) 353-1655 · Fax: (908) 353-0255 · http://www.hollym.com
Published simultaneously in Korea by Hollym Corporation; Publishers at 13-13 Gwancheol-dong, Jongno-gu, Seoul 110-111, Korea
Tel: (02) 735-7551~4 · Fax: (02) 730-5149, 8192 · http://www.hollym.co.kr · ISBN: 1-56591-009-5 · Library of Congress Catalog Card Number: 93-61331 · Printed in Korea

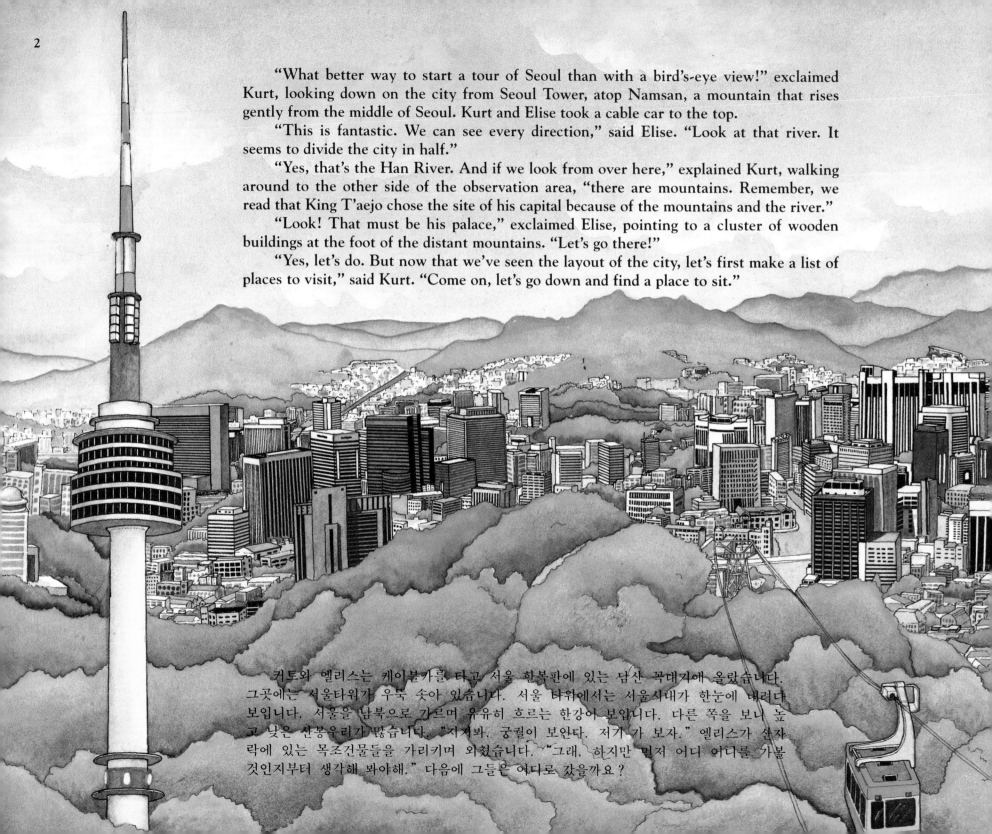

2

"What better way to start a tour of Seoul than with a bird's-eye view!" exclaimed Kurt, looking down on the city from Seoul Tower, atop Namsan, a mountain that rises gently from the middle of Seoul. Kurt and Elise took a cable car to the top.

"This is fantastic. We can see every direction," said Elise. "Look at that river. It seems to divide the city in half."

"Yes, that's the Han River. And if we look from over here," explained Kurt, walking around to the other side of the observation area, "there are mountains. Remember, we read that King T'aejo chose the site of his capital because of the mountains and the river."

"Look! That must be his palace," exclaimed Elise, pointing to a cluster of wooden buildings at the foot of the distant mountains. "Let's go there!"

"Yes, let's do. But now that we've seen the layout of the city, let's first make a list of places to visit," said Kurt. "Come on, let's go down and find a place to sit."

커트와 엘리스는 케이블카를 타고 서울 한복판에 있는 남산 꼭대기에 올랐습니다. 그곳에는 서울타워가 우뚝 솟아 있습니다. 서울 타워에서는 서울시내가 한눈에 내려다 보입니다. 서울을 남북으로 가르며 유유히 흐르는 한강이 보입니다. 다른 쪽을 보니 높고 낮은 산봉우리가 많습니다. "저거봐. 궁궐이 보인다. 저기가 보자." 엘리스가 산자락에 있는 목조건물들을 가리키며 외쳤습니다. "그래. 하지만 먼저 어디 어디를 가볼 것인지부터 생각해 봐야해." 다음에 그들은 어디로 갔을까요?

Kurt and Elise sat on the steps of P'algak-jŏng, an octagonal pavilion near the base of Seoul Tower, and studied their map and guidebook. They decided to first explore the area north of the river, starting with Kyŏngbokkung Palace.

"Let's go," said Elise, getting to her feet. "There's a lot of things to see."

"Race you down the hill!" laughed Kurt as he ran ahead.

커트와 엘리스는 서울타워를 내려와 남산 팔각정 계단에 앉았습니다. 지도와 안내책자를 펼쳐보면서 그들은 경복궁부터 구경하기로 결정했습니다. 경복궁은 볼거리가 많을 것입니다.

4

The throne hall, Kŭnjŏngjŏn, w
Kurt and Elise's first stop inside Kyŏ
bokkung Palace.

"This is the most important bui
ing in the palace," said Elise. "It's whe
the king ruled the nation."

"Wow! Look at the throne! It's
colorful!" exclaimed Kurt. "And look
those carved dragons. They're ever
where."

"Didn't we read that dragon was
symbol of the king?" asked Elise.

"That's right," said Kurt. "Let's lo
for more dragons."

"You see those stone markers?" asked Kurt, pointing to two rows of stone posts in the courtyard. "The guidebook said that's where the officials stood for meeting with the king."

"Look at the roof," said Elise. "The shape matches the mountains."

"Come on," said Kurt, "Let's look at another part of the palace."

경복궁 근정전은 왕좌가 있는 건물로, 왕이 집무를 보던 곳입니다. 그런데 커트는 근정전 앞 뜰에 두 줄로 늘어서 있는 돌이 무엇인지 무척 궁금한가 봅니다. 품계석이라고 하는 이 돌에는 신하들의 지위가 표시되어져 있어서 신하들은 자신의 지위가 씌어진 돌 앞에 서서 왕을 알현하곤 했었습니다. 멀리서 바라본 근정전은 주변의 경치와 조화를 이뤄 더욱 아름답습니다.

On completing their tour of Kyŏngbokkung Palace, Kurt and Elise headed to nearby Ch'ŏngwadae,
the place where the President of Korea resides and performs his official duties.
"The building looks similar to the wooden buildings we saw at the palace," said Elise.
"Those flowers must be Roses of Sharon, Korea's national flower."
"Wow! I wish we were ambassadors," exclaimed Kurt.
"Then we could meet the president!"

커트와 엘리스는 경복궁을 둘러본 후 청와
대로 발길을 옮겼습니다. 청와대에는 대통령이
살고 계시는 곳이며, 대통령 직무와 국가 원수
및 외교 사절이 방문할 때 접견하는 곳입니다.
　　청와대는 전통 목조 구조와 궁궐 양식을 기
본으로 하였으며, 지붕을 청기와로 이어 우아함
과 아름다움이 뛰어난 건물이었습니다.
　　청와대 주위에는 한국의 국화인 무궁화가
곱게 피어 있었습니다.

8

After Ch'ŏngwadae, Kurt and Elise checked their list and headed for Insa-dong. On the way they stopped for lunch.

"It's spicy!" exclaimed Elise after tasting *kimch'i*, spicy fermented cabbage that is served at every meal.

"Try this. It's delicious," said Kurt, wrapping a piece of *bulgogi*, charbroiled marinated beef, in a lettuce leaf and popping it in his mouth.

커트와 엘리스는 청와대를 나와 인사동으로 가면서 점심을 먹었습니다. 엘리스는 한국의 전통음식인 김치를 먹어보았습니다. "휴, 너무 매워." 엘리스의 눈에는 눈물까지 맺혔습니다. 커트는 숯불 위에서 구워낸 불고기를 상추에 싸서 맛있게 먹으면서 엘리스에게도 권했습니다.

After lunch Kurt and Elise walked around Insa-dong, an area packed with art galleries and shops selling antiques, ceramics, old books, paintings, handicrafts and more.

"Oh, Elise! Look at me!" called Kurt, putting on a colorful mask.

"That's great.!" exclaimed Elise, turning around with a mask on too. "Let's buy them! They're fun!"

인사동은 화랑, 골동품 가게, 고서점, 민속 공예품점 따위가 모여 있는 곳입니다. 진열된 물건 하나하나가 커트와 엘리스의 관심을 끌었습니다. 탈을 써 보기도 하면서 재미있는 시간을 가졌습니다.

Next Kurt and Elise visited Chogye-sa, a Buddhist temple a couple of blocks west of Insa-dong. It was Buddha's Birthday so the courtyard was crowded with people of all ages who had come to offer prayers to Buddha in the form of paper lanterns.

"This is fantastic!" exclaimed Elise, looking at the strings of lanterns over her head and in the limbs of the huge Bodhi tree in the temple yard. "There are lanterns of all shapes and sizes and with all kinds of decorations."

"There's even one with a swastika," said Kurt.

"That's not a swastika. That's an ancient Buddhist symbol," explained Elise. "I read it in the guidebook."

"Let's buy a lantern," said Kurt.

Kurt and Elise bought a lantern and wrote their names on it. A monk helped them hang it in the Bodhi tree and then said a prayer for them. Perhaps he prayed that they would learn a lot about Korea.

조계사라는 절에 들른 커트와 엘리스는 눈이 휘둥그레졌습니다. 마침 부처님 오신날을 맞아 조계사 뜰에는 형형색색의 연등이 가득 걸려있고 사람들로 북적거렸기 때문입니다.

커트와 엘리스도 다른 사람들처럼 연등을 사서 그 위에 그들의 이름을 적었습니다. 한 스님의 도움으로 연등을 걸고 부처님께 소원을 빌었습니다. 아마도 한국에 대해 더 많이 알게 해달라고 빌지 않았을까요?

Ch'angdŏkkung, a detached palace to the east of Kyŏngbokkung, was the next stop on Kurt and Elise's tour.

"The buildings look so big and grand," exclaimed Kurt.

"This book says the palace is a good example of Chosŏn wooden architecture and that the buildings were made to blend with the landscape," explained Elise, closing her guidebook.

커트와 엘리스는 창덕궁에 왔습니다. 입구인 돈화문을 지나서 잘 보존된 목조건물들과 아름다운 주변 경관을 감상했습니다. 창덕궁은 경복궁 다음으로 오래된 궁궐입니다.

After touring the palace buildings, Kurt and Elise went to Piwon, a garden
in the northern sector of Ch'angdŏkkung. They walked along the paths and
looked at the many pavilions, ponds and springs.
"You know, this garden was where the king and his family came to rest and
enjoy themselves," said Elise, looking at her guidebook.
"Yes, I guess that's why they called it Secret Garden," replied Kurt.

창덕궁 뒤편에는 비원이라고 하는 정원이 있습니
왕이 휴식을 취하던 곳입니다. 커트와 엘리스는
잡한 서울 시내 한복판에 이렇게 아름답고 조용한
원이 있다는 것이 놀라웠습니다.

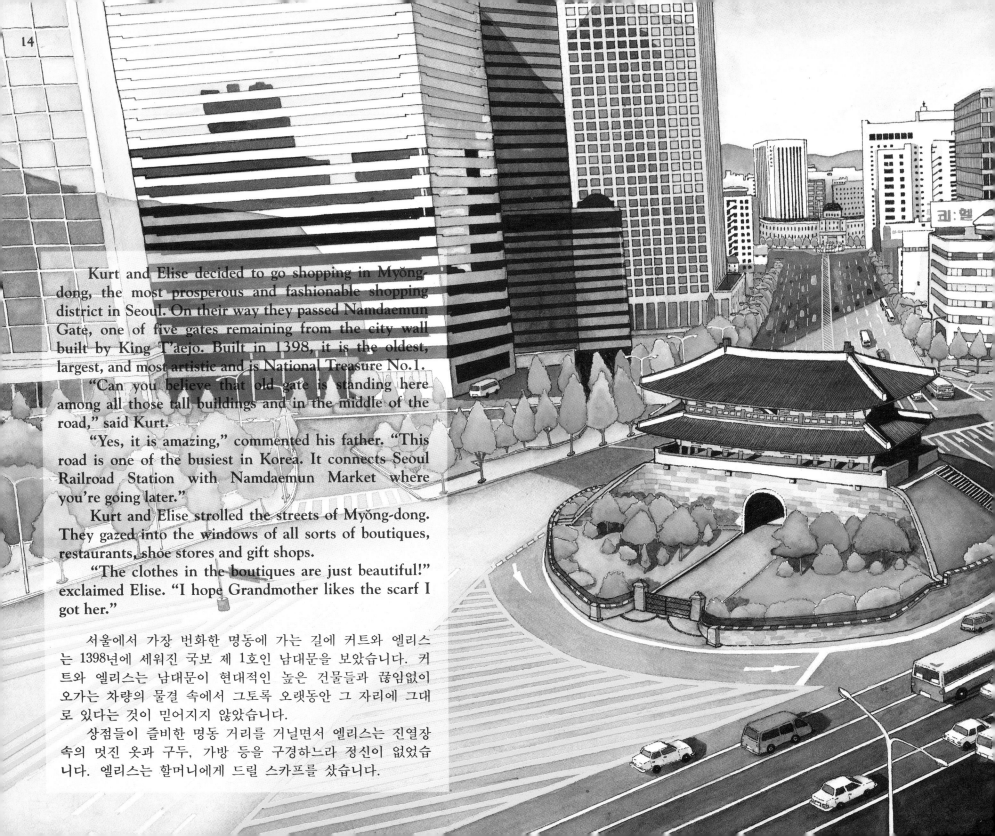

Kurt and Elise decided to go shopping in Myŏng-dong, the most prosperous and fashionable shopping district in Seoul. On their way they passed Namdaemun Gate, one of five gates remaining from the city wall built by King T'aejo. Built in 1398, it is the oldest, largest, and most artistic and is National Treasure No.1.

"Can you believe that old gate is standing here among all those tall buildings and in the middle of the road," said Kurt.

"Yes, it is amazing," commented his father. "This road is one of the busiest in Korea. It connects Seoul Railroad Station with Namdaemun Market where you're going later."

Kurt and Elise strolled the streets of Myŏng-dong. They gazed into the windows of all sorts of boutiques, restaurants, shoe stores and gift shops.

"The clothes in the boutiques are just beautiful!" exclaimed Elise. "I hope Grandmother likes the scarf I got her."

서울에서 가장 번화한 명동에 가는 길에 커트와 엘리스는 1398년에 세워진 국보 제 1호인 남대문을 보았습니다. 커트와 엘리스는 남대문이 현대적인 높은 건물들과 끊임없이 오가는 차량의 물결 속에서 그토록 오랫동안 그 자리에 그대로 있다는 것이 믿어지지 않았습니다.

상점들이 즐비한 명동 거리를 거닐면서 엘리스는 진열장속의 멋진 옷과 구두, 가방 등을 구경하느라 정신이 없었습니다. 엘리스는 할머니에게 드릴 스카프를 샀습니다.

돼지머리고기

떡국

On the way to their hotel, Kurt and Eli
stopped at Namdaemun Market, which is nam
for the nearby Namdaemun Gate. The vast ma
ket was crowded with shoppers and vendors se
ing everything from gloves and sunglasses to ba
and pig's heads.

남대문 옆에는 남대문 시장이 있습니다. 남대
시장에는 없는 것이 없는 것 같았습니다.

Kurt and Elise sampled fish cakes on sticks at one of the many food stalls. They looked at bags and hats, toys and shoes, and much more. They even tried on *hanbok*, Korea's traditional clothes.

"What a great place!" exclaimed Kurt as they left the market. "Shopping there is fun!"

커트와 엘리스는 남대문시장 구석구석을 구경했습니다. 정말 재미있었습니다. 물건 값도 싼 것 같았습니다. 활기찬 남대문 시장은 쇼핑하기에 아주 좋은 곳이라고 생각했습니다.

Kurt and Elise decided to take a boat ride on the Han River before beginning their tour of the south side.

"That's certainly a tall building," said Kurt, looking up at the nearby 63 Building as the boat pulled away from the dock.

"Maybe we should add it to our list. I read it has a huge aquarium in the bottom and an observation tower on top," replied Elise.

"Look at those kids playing baseball," Kurt shouted, pointing to the shore. "Look! Basketball courts, soccer fields..."

"A swimming pool!" exclaimed Elise. "Wow! There are parks on both sides of the river. Look at all the picnickers!"

"See all the apartment buildings. I guess the people living in them really enjoy those parks."

"And the river," added Elise. "They can fish and water-ski and wind-surf...."

커트와 엘리스는 이제 서울의 강남지역을 구경할 계획을 세우면서 우선 한강의 유람선을 타기로 했습니다. 시원한 강바람을 맞으며 강변의 경치를 구경했습니다. 63빌딩도 보였습니다. 그곳에는 대형 수족관과 전망대가 있어 찾아가볼 계획을 세웠습니다. 강변 잔디밭에서는 아이들이 공놀이를 즐기고 있었습니다. 농구장, 축구장, 수영장도 있고…, 소풍 나온 사람들도 여기저기 눈에 띄었습니다. 모두가 행복해 보였습니다.

"저기 아파트들 좀 봐." 많은 아파트들이 한강을 굽어보며 강변에 솟아 있었습니다. 커트와 엘리스는 한강과 그 주변의 모든 것들을 쉽게 즐길 수 있는 그 아파트에 사는 사람들이 부러웠습니다.

In about an hour, the boat docked at Chamshil, the site of the Olympic Stadium and the huge Lotte World amusement park.

Kurt and Elise strolled around a riverside park near the boat dock. Kurt played baseball and then they watched a girl painting a river scene. They looked at flowers, watched some fishermen, and waved to passing boats and wind surfers.

"We'll have to visit some more of the riverside parks," declared Kurt as they left the park. "They're fun!"

한 시간 쯤 유람선을 타고 도착한 곳은 올림픽 경기장과 롯데월드가 있는 잠실이었습니다. 커트와 엘리스는 선착장 주변을 산책하며 잔디밭에서 직접 야구도 해 보았습니다. 낚시와 윈드서핑을 즐기는 사람들도 있었습니다. 커트와 엘리스도 그들 속에 끼고 싶었습니다.

The next day Kurt and Elise went to Lotte World to visit Lotte World Adventure, the world's largest indoor theme park, and Magic Island, an outdoor amusement park.
"Wow! We can see all the rides from here!" cried Kurt, as he and Elise soared up in a balloon ride over Magic Island.
"There's the monorail!" pointed Elise. "Let's ride that back into Lotte World Adventure!"
"Yes, I want to go back in there. We didn't ride everything," replied Kurt.
"And we didn't see all the shows," added Elise.

다음날 커트와 엘리스는 롯데월드와 롯데월드 어드밴처를 구경했습니다. 호수 위에 떠 있는 섬, 매직 아일랜드에선 놀이 기구도 즐겼습니다. 모노레일 을 타고 롯데월드 어드밴처로 다시 들어가서 재미있는 쇼도 구경했습니다.

Kurt and Elise left Magic Island and went next door to the Seoul Norimadang, an outdoor theater for traditional Korean dance, music and theater performances.

"This music makes me feel like dancing," exclaimed Kurt as they watched a performance of *nong-ak*, farmer's dance.

"You're not the only one!" replied Elise and pointed to some people in the audience. "It's very loud and exciting!"

"And quite different from our music," said Kurt.

롯데월드 옆에 있는 서울놀이마당은 한국의 전통 춤과 노래를 공연하는 야외 극장입니다. "절로 흥이 나는 걸." 농악 공연을 보며 커트가 말하자, "나도 그래, 어깨가 들썩거리는데." 라며 엘리스가 맞장구를 쳤습니다. 그들은 낯설지만 흥겨운 한국의 춤과 음악에 흠뻑 취했습니다.

Kurt and Elise watched a performance by four musicians called *samulnori*. It was followed by a masked dance performance.

"That's like the mask I bought!" exclaimed Kurt as the performers entered the performance area.

"And there's one like mine!" cried Elise.

As they left the Norimadang, Kurt said, "That was great. We can wear our masks and perform for our friends. I bet they would like Korean music and dance."

장고, 북, 징, 꽹과리등 한국의 전통악기 네가지가 어우러져 한판 신명나게 펼쳐지는 사물놀이 공연은 정말 잊을 수 없는 경험이었습니다. 탈춤 역시 커트와 엘리스에게는 흥미로웠습니다. 인사동에서 샀던 탈을 쓰고 친구들에게 탈춤을 춰 보일 생각을 하니 신이 났습니다. 커트와 엘리스의 친구들 역시 탈춤을 좋아할 것입니다.

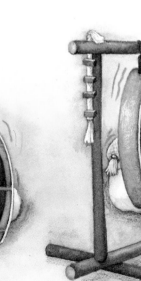

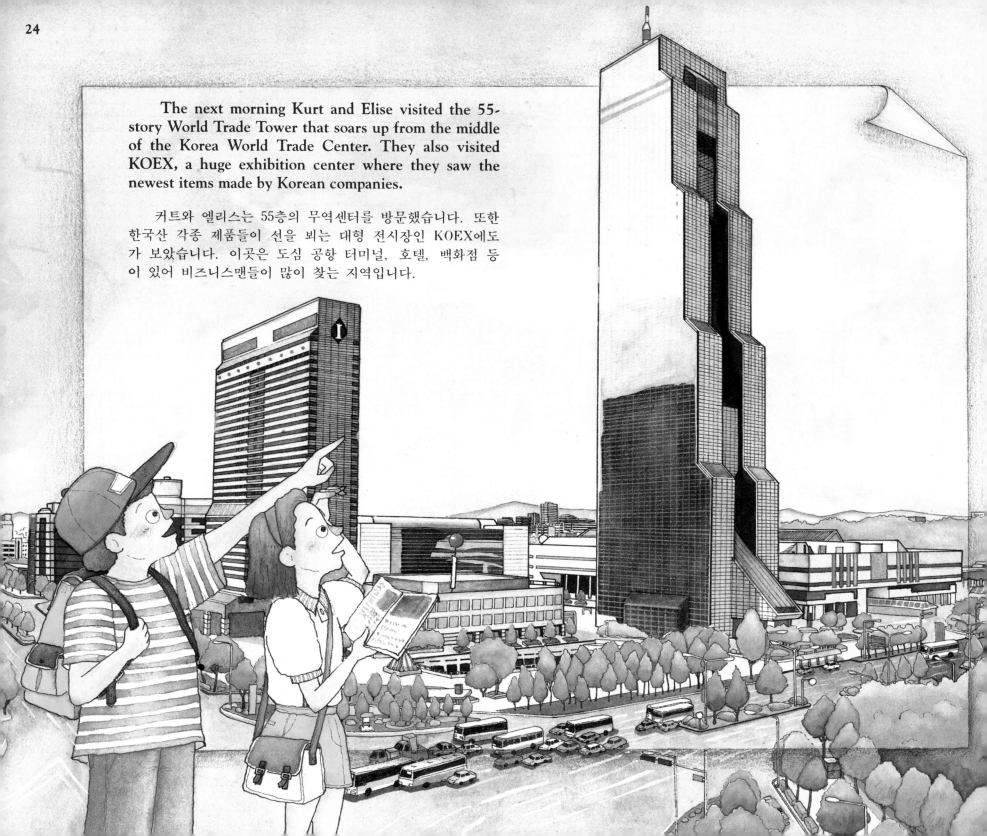

The next morning Kurt and Elise visited the 55-story World Trade Tower that soars up from the middle of the Korea World Trade Center. They also visited KOEX, a huge exhibition center where they saw the newest items made by Korean companies.

커트와 엘리스는 55층의 무역센터를 방문했습니다. 또한 한국산 각종 제품들이 선을 뵈는 대형 전시장인 KOEX에도 가 보았습니다. 이곳은 도심 공항 터미널, 호텔, 백화점 등이 있어 비즈니스맨들이 많이 찾는 지역입니다.

In the afternoon Kurt and Elise went to the Seoul Arts Center.

"Wow! These buildings are certainly big and modern looking!" exclaimed Kurt.

"There is a hall for only opera, a concert hall, an art gallery, a festival hall, an outdoor theater and a calligraphy hall," Elise read from her guidebook.

"What's calligraphy?" asked Kurt.

"I think it is brush writing," replied Elise.

"Then let's go to the calligraphy hall," said Kurt.

예술의 전당을 찾은 커트와 앨러스는 건물이 무척 아름답다고 생각했습니다. 이곳은 오페라 하우스, 콘서트홀, 음악당, 국악당, 서예관 등이 있는 종합 문화예술 공연장입니다.

Kurt wanted to see some Korean sports so they went to a wrestling match.
"What is this kind of wrestling called?" asked Elise.
"*Ssirŭm*," replied Kurt. "I read about it in my guidebook. It's over 1500 years old."
"How can you tell the winner from the loser?" asked Elise.
"The loser," explained Kurt, "is the first wrestler to touch the ground with any part of his body, other than his feet."

커트와 엘리스는 한국의 민속 경기인 씨름을 보기 위해 씨름 경기장을 찾았습니다. 씨름은 1,500년 이상 한국인들이 즐겨온 운동입니다. 서로 상대 선수의 허리에 매어진 샅바를 잡고 각종 기술을 걸어 상대를 모래판에 쓰러뜨리면 이기는 경기입니다.

Kurt and Elise visited a *t'aekwondo* class. They were surprised to learn that *t'aekwondo* was developed in Korea.

"Look, Elise! I can kick, too!" exclaimed Kurt, trying to imitate the students.

"I bet you can't break boards like that boy," teased Elise, as they watched a boy break board after board with his feet.

태권도장을 들어간 커트와 엘리스는 세계인이 함께 하는 태권도가 한국에서 시작된 운동경기라는 사실을 알고는 놀랐습니다. 태권도는 심신을 단련시키는 운동으로 한국의 어린이와 청소년들에게 인기가 높습니다. 한 소년이 맨주먹으로 합판을 연속적으로 격파하는 것을 본 커트와 엘리스는 입을 다물지 못했습니다.

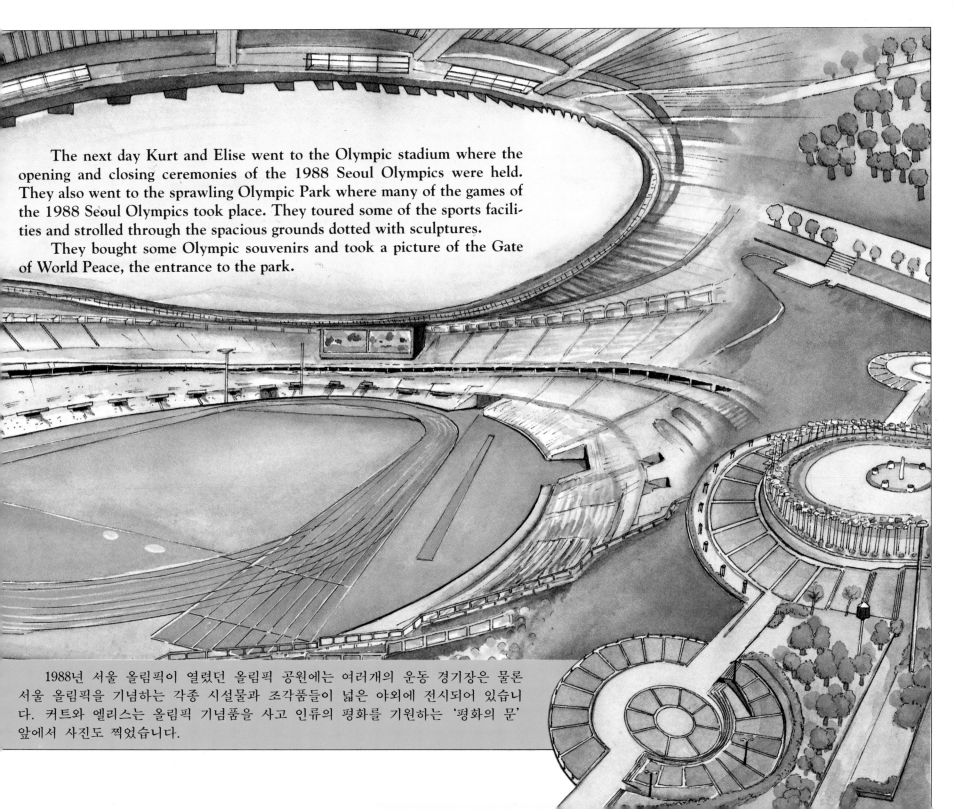

The next day Kurt and Elise went to the Olympic stadium where the opening and closing ceremonies of the 1988 Seoul Olympics were held. They also went to the sprawling Olympic Park where many of the games of the 1988 Seoul Olympics took place. They toured some of the sports facilities and strolled through the spacious grounds dotted with sculptures.

They bought some Olympic souvenirs and took a picture of the Gate of World Peace, the entrance to the park.

1988년 서울 올림픽이 열렸던 올림픽 공원에는 여러개의 운동 경기장은 물론 서울 올림픽을 기념하는 각종 시설물과 조각품들이 넓은 야외에 전시되어 있습니다. 커트와 엘리스는 올림픽 기념품을 사고 인류의 평화를 기원하는 '평화의 문' 앞에서 사진도 찍었습니다.

On their last night in Seoul, Kurt and Elise's family visited the 63 Building to have a night view of the city.

"Wow! This is fantastic!" exclaimed Kurt, as he looked down on Seoul from the observation tower on the sixtieth floor. "There are lights as far as one can see!"

"I like the river!" declared Elise, looking at the lights glistening on the water. "It looks like it is celebrating Seoul's birthday."

서울에서의 마지막 밤. 커트와 엘리스는 가족들과 함께 63빌딩에 가서 서울의 야경을 즐겼습니다. 60층에 있는 전망대에서 바라본 서울의 밤은 환상적이었습니다. 엘리스는 불빛에 반짝거리는 한강의 잔물결들이 마치 서울의 생일을 축하하는 것 같다고 말했습니다.

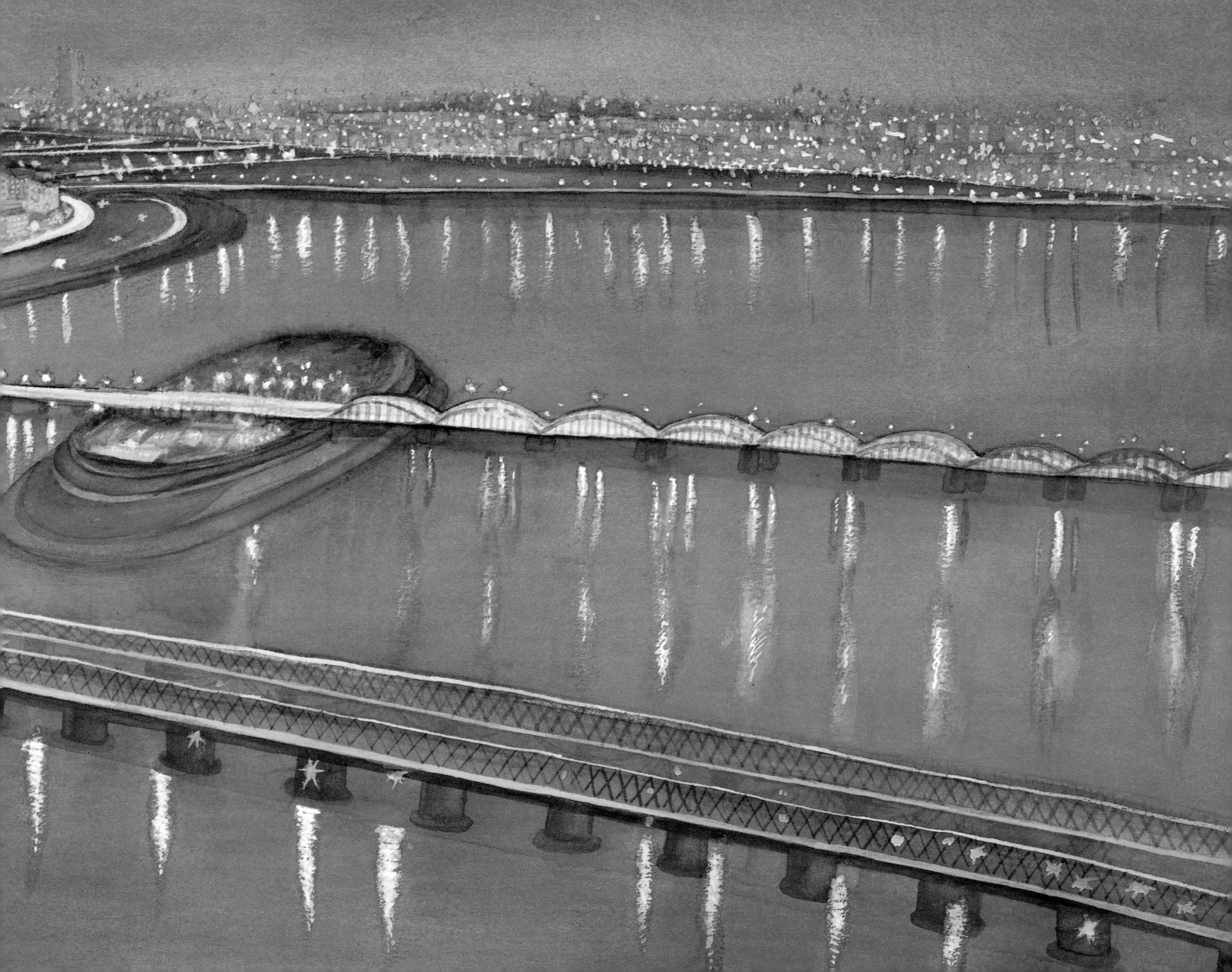

Let's Visit Korea

펴낸날 / 1993년 10월 4일 제1판 1쇄
         2005년 11월 15일 제1판 6쇄
펴낸이 / 임상백
펴낸곳 / (주)한림출판사
주소 / 서울 특별시 종로구 관철동 13-13
전화 / (02)735-7551~4 팩시밀리 (02) 730-5149
홈페이지 / www.hollym.co.kr

미국발행처 / Hollym International Corp.
18 Donald Place Elizabeth, NJ 07208, U.S.A.
Tel / (908)353-1655 Fax (908)353-0255
http://www.hollym.co.kr
ISBN 1-56591-009-5